Paper Creations

Merry Christmas ORIGAMI

Duy & Tramy Nguyen

STERLING

New York / London
www.sterlingpublishing.com

STERLING and the distinctive Sterling logo are registered trademarks
of Sterling Publishing Co., Inc.

2 4 6 8 10 9 7 5 3 1

Published by Sterling Publishing Co., Inc.
387 Park Avenue South, New York, NY 10016

© 2008 by Sterling Publishing Co., Inc.

Some of the projects in this book have also appeared in
Holiday Origami on the Flip Side © 2008 by Duy & Tramy Nguyen

Distributed in Canada by Sterling Publishing
c/o Canadian Manda Group, 165 Dufferin Street
Toronto, Ontario, Canada M6K 3H6
Distributed in the United Kingdom by GMC Distribution Services
Castle Place, 166 High Street, Lewes, East Sussex, England BN7 1XU
Distributed in Australia by Capricorn Link (Australia) Pty. Ltd.
P.O. Box 704, Windsor, NSW 2756, Australia

Design by Beth Nori

Sterling ISBN 978-1-4027-5081-6

For information about custom editions, special sales, premium and
corporate purchases, please contact Sterling Special Sales
Department at 800-805-5489 or specialsales@sterlingpublishing.com.

CONTENTS

❄ BASIC INSTRUCTIONS

Paper

The best origami paper will be very thin, keep a crease well, and fold flat. It can be plain white paper, solid-color paper, or wrapping paper with a design only on one side. Regular typing paper may be too heavy to allow the many tight folds needed for some figures. Be aware, too, that some kinds of paper may stretch slightly, either in length or in width, and this may cause a problem in paper folding. Packets of paper especially for use in origami are available from craft and hobby shops.

Unless otherwise indicated, the paper customarily used in creating these forms is square, 15 by 15 centimeters or approximately 6 by 6 inches. Some forms may call for half a square, i.e., 3 by 6 inches or, cut diagonally, a triangle. A few origami forms require a more rectangular size or a longer piece of paper. For those who are learning and have a problem getting their fingers to work tight folds, larger sizes of paper can be used. Actually, any size paper squares can be used—slightly larger figures are easier to make than overly small ones. The paper provided within this gift set is 6 by 6 inches, easy to work with for origami novices.

Glue

Use an easy-flowing but not loose paper glue. Use it sparingly; you don't want to soak the paper. A toothpick makes a good applicator. Allow the glued form time to dry. Avoid using stick glue, as the application pressure needed (especially if the stick has become dry) can damage your figure.

Technique

Fold with care. Position the paper, especially at corners, precisely and see that the edges line up before creasing a fold. Once you are sure of the fold, use a fingernail to make a clean, flat crease. Don't get discouraged with your first efforts. In time, what your mind can create, your fingers can fashion.

❄ SYMBOLS & LINES

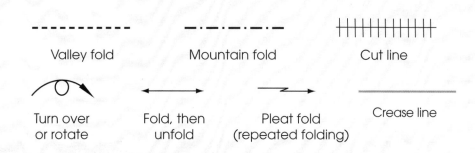

Valley fold

Mountain fold

Cut line

Turn over
or rotate

Fold, then
unfold

Pleat fold
(repeated folding)

Crease line

❄ SQUARING OFF PAPER

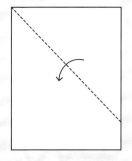

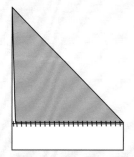

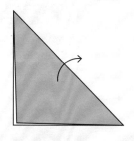

1. Take a rectangular
sheet and valley
fold diagonally.

2. Cut off excess on
short side as shown.

3. Unfold. Sheet is
square.

BASIC FOLDS

Kite Fold

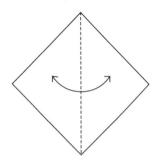

1. Fold and unfold a square diagonally, making a center crease.

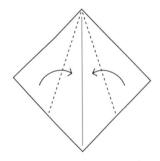

2. Fold both sides in to the center crease.

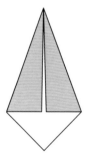

3. This is a kite fold.

Valley Fold

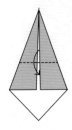

1. Start with a kite fold. Fold form toward you (forward), making a "valley."

2. This is a valley fold.

Mountain Fold

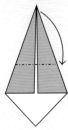

1. Start with a kite fold. Fold form away from you (backward), making a "mountain."

2. This is a mountain fold.

Inside Reverse Fold

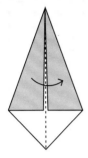

1. Starting here with a kite, valley fold kite closed.

2. Valley fold as marked to crease, then unfold.

3. Pull tip in direction of arrow.

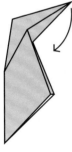

4. Appearance before completion.

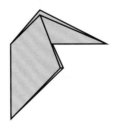

5. This is an inside reverse fold.

Outside Reverse Fold

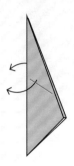

1. Start with a closed kite fold. Valley fold and unfold.

2. Fold inside out as shown by arrows.

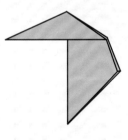

3. Continue pulling tip in direction of arrows.

4. This is an outside reverse fold.

Pleat Fold

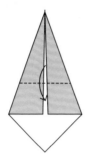

1. Start with a kite fold. Valley fold.

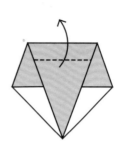

2. Valley fold back.

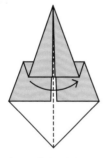

3. This is a pleat fold. Valley fold in half.

4. You've made a pleat fold form.

Pleat Fold Reverse

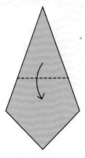

1. Start with a kite fold. Turn over and valley fold.

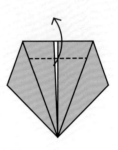

2. Valley fold back.

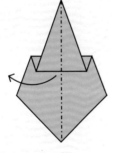

3. This is a pleat fold reverse. Mountain fold in half.

4. This is a pleat fold reverse form.

Squash Fold I

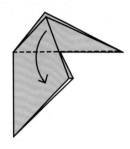 

1. Start with an inside reverse fold. Valley fold front layer.

2. This is a squash fold I.

Squash Fold II

1. Start with a closed kite fold. Valley fold.

2. Open in direction of the arrow.

3. Open in direction of the arrows.

4. This is a squash fold II.

Inside Crimp Fold

 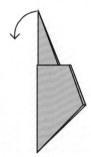 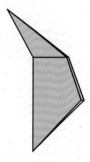

1. Start with a closed kite fold. Pleat fold.

2. Pull tip in direction of the arrow.

3. This is an inside crimp fold.

Outside Crimp Fold

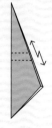  

1. Start with a closed kite fold. Pleat fold and unfold.

2. Make mountain and valley folds both front and back.

3. This is an outside crimp fold.

❄ BASE FOLDS

Base folds are basic forms that do not in themselves produce origami, but serve as a basis, or jumping-off point, for a number of creative origami figures—some quite complex. As when beginning other crafts, learning to fold these base folds is not the most exciting part of origami. They are, however, easy to do, and will help you with your technique. They also quickly become rote, so much so that you can do many using different-colored papers while you are watching television or your mind is elsewhere. With completed base folds handy, if you want to quickly work up a form or are suddenly inspired with an idea for an original, unique figure, you can select an appropriate base fold and swiftly bring a new creation to life.

Base Fold I

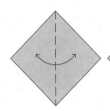 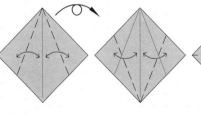 

1. Valley fold, then unfold.

2. Make valley folds, then unfold. Rotate.

3. Make valley folds, then unfold.

4. Pinch corners of square together and fold inward.

5. Completed Base Fold I.

Base Fold II

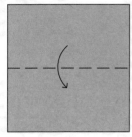

1. Valley fold.

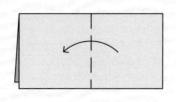

2. Valley fold.

3. Squash fold.

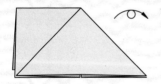

4. Turn over.

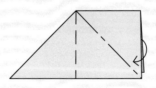

5. Squash fold.

6. Completed Base Fold II.

Base Fold III

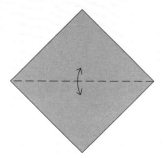

1. Valley fold.

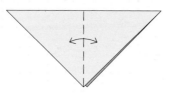

2. Valley fold and unfold.

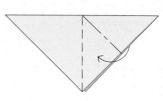

3. Squash fold.

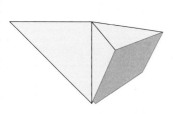

4. Appearance before completion.

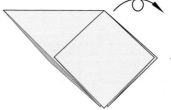

5. Turn over.

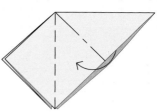

6. Squash fold.

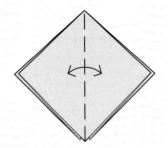

7. Valley fold and unfold.

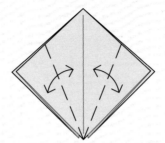

8. Make valley folds, then unfold.

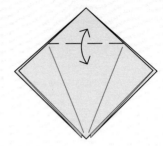

9. Valley fold and unfold.

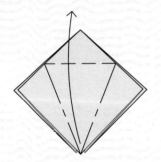

10. Pull in direction of arrow, folding inward at sides.

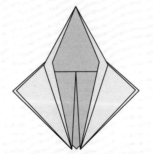

11. Appearance before completion.

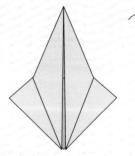

12. Turn over.

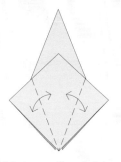

13. Make valley folds, then unfold.

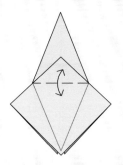

14. Valley fold, then unfold.

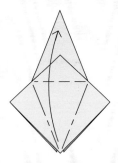

15. Repeat step 10, again pulling in direction of arrow.

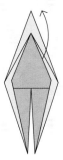

16. Appearance before completion.

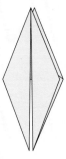

17. Completed Base Fold III.

Base Fold IV

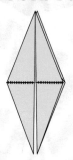

1. Start with Base Fold III. Cut first layer only as shown.

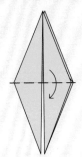

2. Valley fold first layer.

3. Turn over.

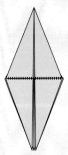

4. Cut first layer only as shown.

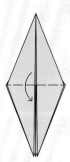

5. Valley fold first layer.

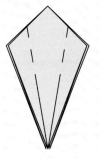

6. Make inside reverse folds.

7. Turn over.

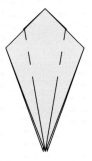

8. Make inside reverse folds.

9. Completed Base Fold IV.

❄ CROSS

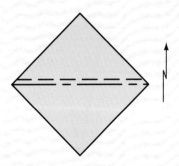

1. Pleat fold.

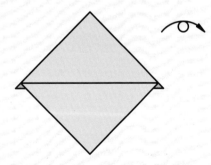

2. Turn over.

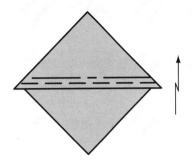

3. Pleat fold.

4. Turn over.

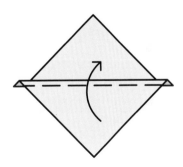

5. Valley fold.

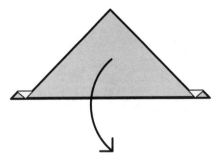

6. Valley fold the front layer only.

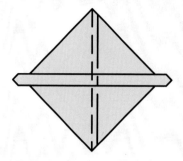

7. Pleat fold.

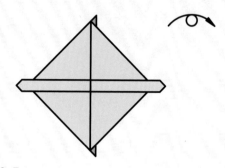

8. Turn over.

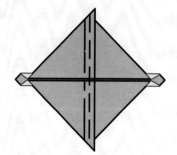

9. Pleat fold.

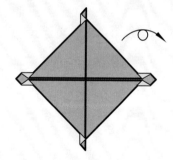

10. Turn over.

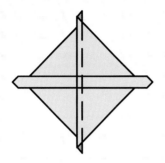

11. Valley fold.

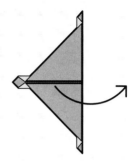

12. Valley fold.

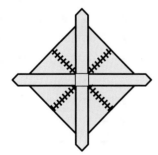

13. Make cuts as shown.

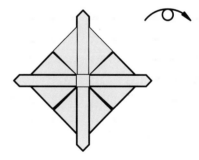

14. Turn over.

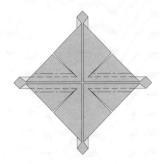

15. Make pleat folds.

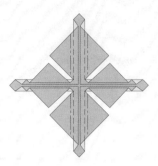

16. Make pleat folds.

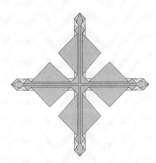

17. Make valley folds.

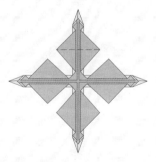

18. Make valley fold.

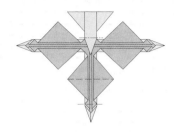

19. Mountain fold, then make valley folds.

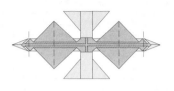

20. Repeat steps 18 and 19.

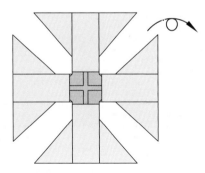

21. Turn over.

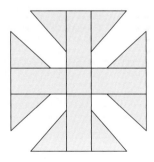

22. Completed Cross.

1. Valley fold in half.

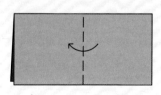

2. Valley fold in half.

3. Valley fold, then unfold.

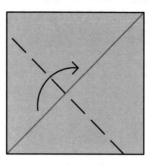

4. Valley fold the front layer only.

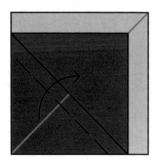

5. Valley fold the front layer only.

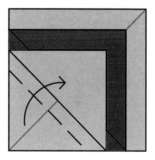

6. Valley fold the front layer only.

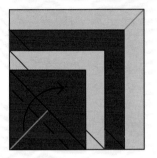

7. Valley fold the front layer only.

8. Rotate.

9. Completed step 8.

10. Repeat steps 1 through 9 four times to complete 4 additional pieces.

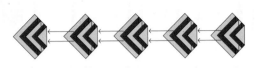

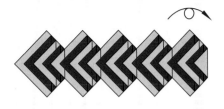

11. Connect the 5 pieces by inserting one into another as shown and apply glue to hold.

12. Turn over.

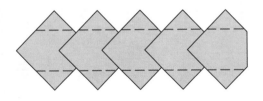

13. Make valley folds.

14. Make valley folds.

15. Valley fold in half.

16. Inside reverse fold, then rotate.

17. Outside reverse fold.

18. Inside reverse fold.

19. Completed Candy Cane.

❄ WREATH

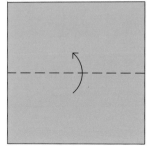

1. Valley fold in half.

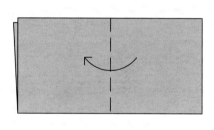

2. Valley fold in half.

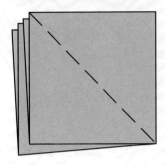

3. Valley fold.

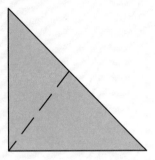

4. Outside reverse fold the front layer only.

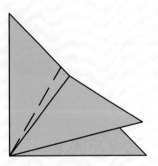

5. Outside reverse fold the front layer only.

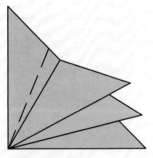

6. Outside reverse fold the front layer only.

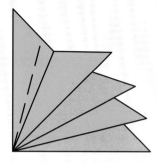

7. Outside reverse fold.

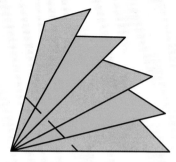

8. Valley fold the front layer only.

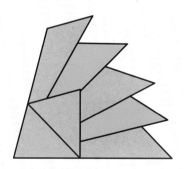

9. Completed Part I.

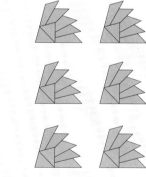

10. Repeat steps 1 through 8 for a total of six pieces.

11. Insert one piece into another as shown and glue to hold.

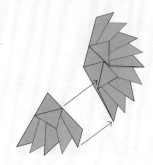

12. Insert a third piece into the first two as shown and glue to hold.

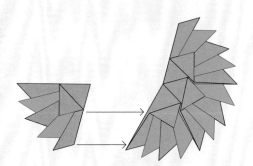

13. Insert a fourth piece into the first three as shown and glue to hold.

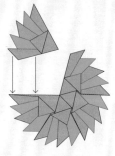

14. Insert a fifth piece into the first four as shown and glue to hold.

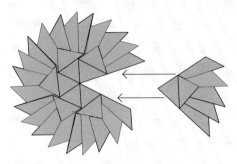

15. Insert the final piece into the first five as shown and glue to hold.

16. Valley fold all center layers.

17. Completed Wreath.

BOW

1. Start with Base Fold I. Mountain fold in half.

2. Inside reverse fold both sides.

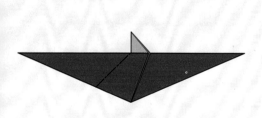

3. Inside reverse fold.

4. Valley fold both sides.

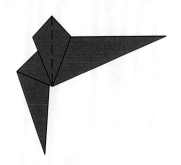

5. Valley fold both sides.

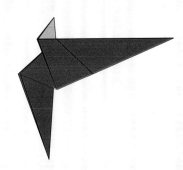

6. Inside reverse fold.

7. Valley fold both sides.

8. Open flaps.

9. Cut both sides as shown.

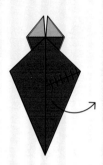

10. Cut as shown, then valley fold.

11. Valley fold.

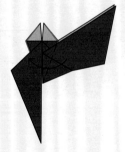

12. Valley fold.

13. Valley fold both sides.

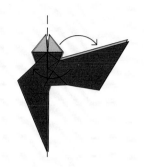

14. Open flaps.

15. Make squash folds.

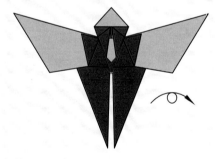

16. Turn over.

17. Make cuts to top layer as shown, then make valley folds.

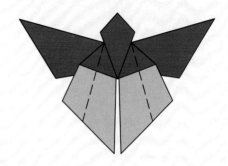

18. Make valley folds.

19. Make squash folds.

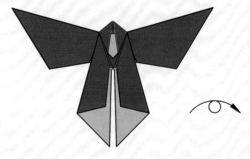

20. Turn over.

21. Without creasing, gently valley fold the tips to the center and glue to hold.

22. Completed Bow.

23. Glue Bow onto Wreath.

24. Completed Wreath with Bow.

1. Start with Base Fold IV. Cut as shown, then valley fold the front layer only.

2. Valley fold.

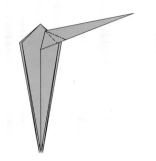

3. Squash fold.

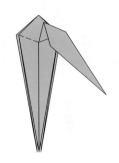

4. Valley fold the front layer only.

5. Valley fold.

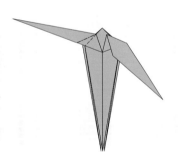

6. Squash fold.

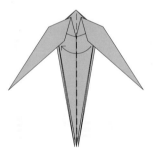

7. Valley fold the front layer only.

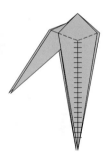

8. Repeat steps 1 through 6.

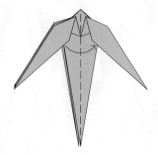

9. Valley fold the front layer only.

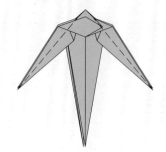

10. Make valley folds.

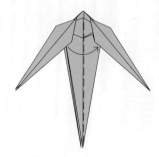

11. Valley fold the front layer only.

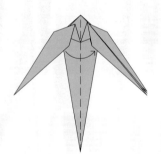

12. Valley fold.

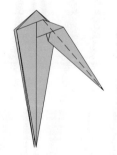

13. Valley fold.

14. Valley fold the front layer only.

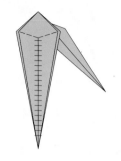

15. Repeat steps 1 through 6.

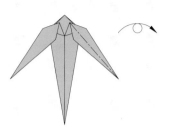

16. Mountain fold, then turn over.

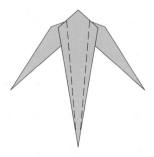

17. Make valley folds.

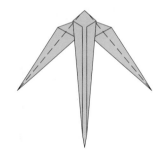

18. Make valley folds.

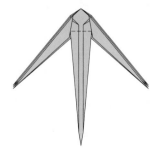

19. Valley fold.

20. Valley fold to open leaves.

21. Inside reverse fold.

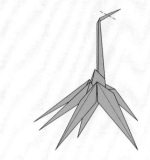

22. Outside reverse fold.

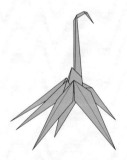

23. Completed Mistletoe.

❄ STAR ORNAMENT

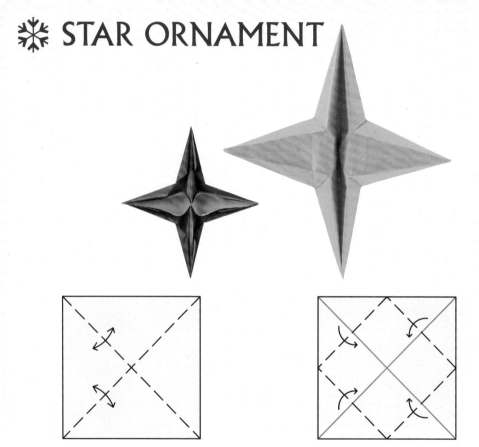

1. Make valley folds, then unfold.

2. Make valley folds.

3. Valley fold in half.

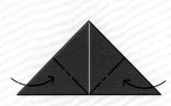

4. Make squash folds on both sides.

5. Make valley folds, then unfold.

6. Pull and fold.

7. Appearance before completion.

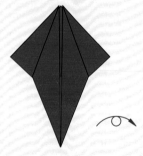

8. Turn over.

9. Repeat steps 5 and 6.

10. Make cuts as shown, then make mountain folds.

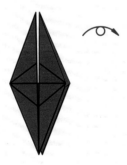

11. Turn over.

12. Make cuts as shown, then make mountain folds.

13. Valley fold both sides.

14. Inside reverse fold all sides.

15. Pull to open.

16. Appearance before completion.

17. Completed Star Ornament.

❄ DIAMOND ORNAMENT

Part I

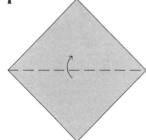

1. Valley fold in half.

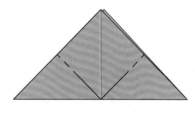

2. Make inside reverse folds.

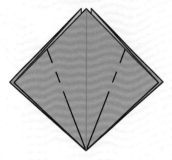

3. Make inside reverse folds, front layer only.

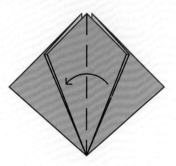

4. Valley fold the front layer only.

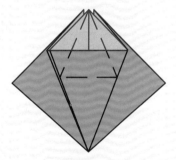

5. Make valley folds, then unfold.

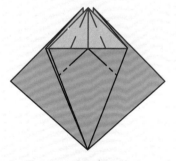

6. Reverse fold both sides.

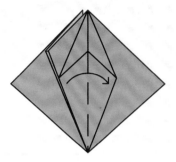

7. Valley fold the front layer only.

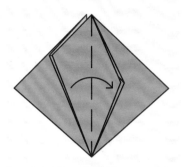

8. Valley fold the front layer only.

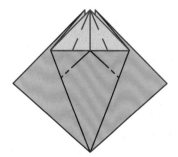

9. Repeat steps 5 and 6.

10. Valley fold.

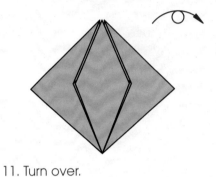

11. Turn over.

12. Make inside reverse folds.

13. Valley fold the front layer only.

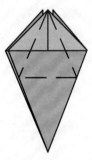

14. Make valley folds, then unfold.

15. Repeat steps 5 and 6.

16. Valley fold the front layer only.

17. Valley fold the front layer only.

18. Repeat steps 5 and 6.

19. Valley fold the front layer only.

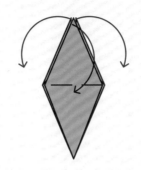

20. Pull to open all sides.

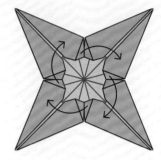

21. Push down.

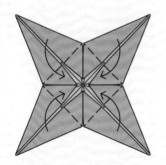

22. Valley fold all sides up and in.

23. Completed Part I.

Part II

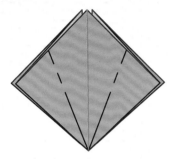

1. Start with step 3 of Part I. Make inside reverse folds.

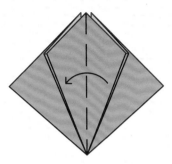

2. Valley fold the front layer only.

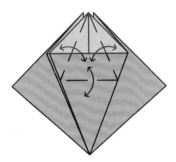

3. Make valley folds, then unfold.

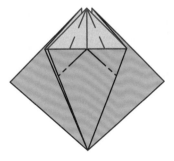

4. Reverse fold both sides.

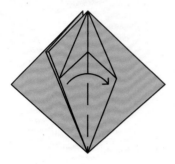

5. Valley fold the front layer only.

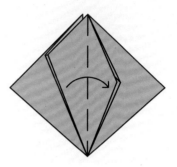

6. Valley fold the front layer only.

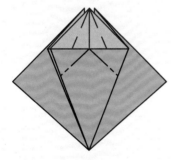

7. Repeat steps 3 and 4.

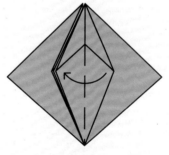

8. Valley fold the front layer only.

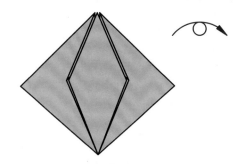

9. Turn over.

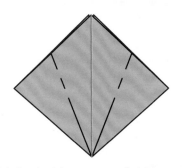

10. Make inside reverse folds.

11. Valley fold the front layer only.

12. Make valley folds, then unfold.

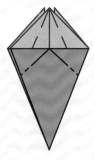

13. Repeat steps 3 and 4.

14. Valley fold the front layer only.

15. Valley fold the front layer only.

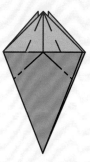

16. Repeat steps 3 and 4.

17. Valley fold the front layer only.

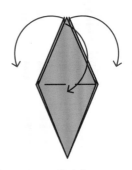

18. Pull to open all sides.

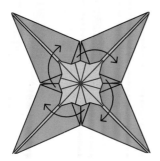

19. Push down.

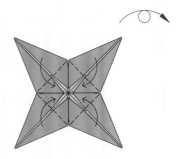

20. Valley fold all sides up and in, then rotate model.

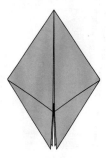

21. Completed Part II.

22. Insert Part II into Part I as shown and glue to hold.

23. Completed Diamond Ornament.

❄ SANTA CLAUS

Part I

1. Start with Base Fold III. Make inside reverse folds.

2. Cut the front layer only as shown, then make valley folds.

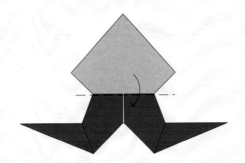

3. Valley fold.

4. Make cuts as shown.

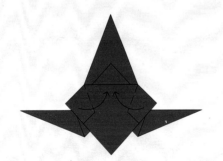

5. Make valley folds.

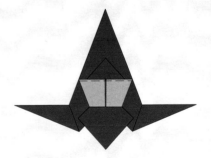

6. Valley fold.

7. Pleat fold.

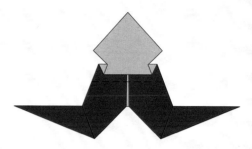

8. Valley fold.

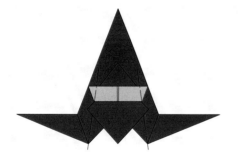

9. Make mountain folds.

10. Turn over.

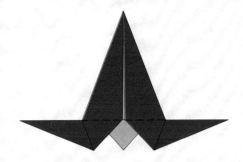

11. Valley fold front layer only.

12. Make valley folds.

13. Valley fold in half.

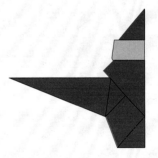

14. Inside reverse fold.

15. Valley fold both arms.

16. Turn over.

17. Mountain fold, then color beard white.

18. Completed Part I.

Part II

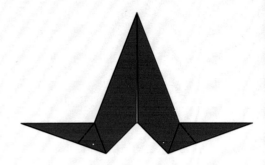

1. Start with Base Fold III. Make inside reverse folds.

2. Make inside reverse folds.

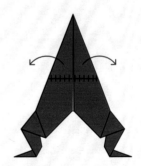

3. Make inside reverse folds.

4. Make cuts as shown, then make valley folds.

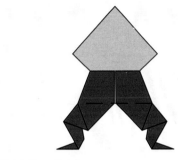

5. Valley fold.

6. Valley fold.

7. Make valley folds.

8. Valley fold.

9. Valley fold.

10. Turn over.

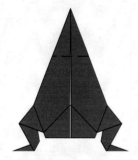

11. Valley fold.

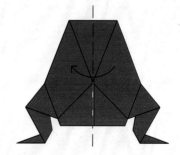

12. Valley fold in half to complete Part II.

13. Insert Part II into Part I as shown and apply glue to hold.

14. Pull and fold both feet.

15. Pull and fold hand.

16. Completed Part II assembly.

Part III

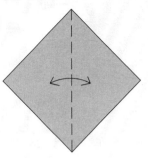

1. Valley fold, then unfold.

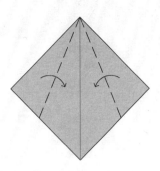

2. Make valley folds.

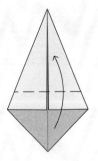

3. Valley fold.

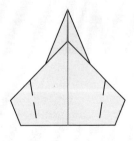

4. Make valley folds.

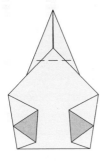

5. Valley fold.

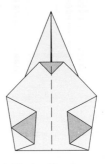

6. Valley fold in half.

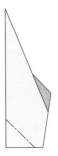

7. Inside reverse fold.

8. Mountain fold the front layer only.

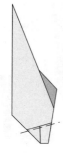

9. Valley fold the back.

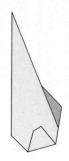

10. Hide flap behind.

11. Outside reverse fold.

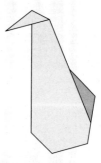

12. Completed Part III.

13. Join Part III to Parts I and II as shown and apply glue to hold.

14. Add color to Santa's boots, if desired.

15. Completed Santa Claus.

❄ REINDEER

Part I

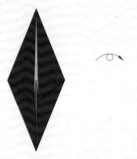

1. Start with Base Fold I. Turn over.

2. Valley fold.

3. Make valley folds.

4. Make valley folds.

5. Make mountain folds.

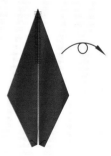

6. Cut top flap, then turn over.

7. Mountain fold top layer only.

8. Mountain fold top layer only.

9. Mountain fold in half.

10. Outside reverse fold top layer only.

11. Cut as shown, then unfold.

12. Make cuts as shown.

13. Cut as shown.

14. Valley fold flap.

15. Valley fold.

16. Add color to the nose, if desired, then turn over.

17. Make cut as shown.

18. Valley fold flap.

19. Valley fold.

20. Completed Part I.

Part II

1. Start with Base Fold I. Make cuts as shown.

2. Make valley folds.

3. Make outside reverse folds.

4. Mountain fold in half.

5. Valley fold.

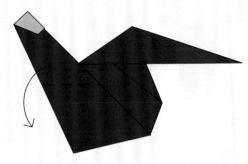

6. Valley fold both front and back.

7. Add color, if desired.

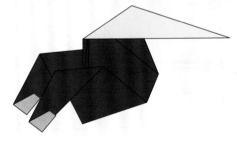

8. Completed Part II.

9. Insert Part I into Part II and apply glue to hold.

10. Valley fold both front and back.

11. Mountain fold.

12. Valley fold the back.

13. Completed Reindeer.

❄ GIFT BOX

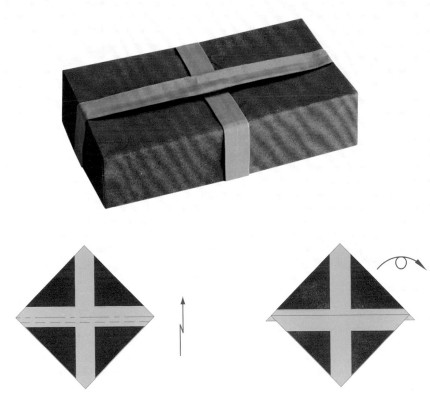

1. Add a pre-cut strip as shown and apply glue to hold, or color a strip onto your paper. Pleat fold.

2. Turn over.

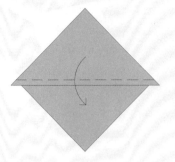

3. Valley fold.

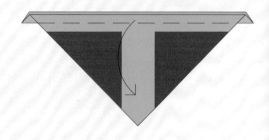

4. Valley fold.

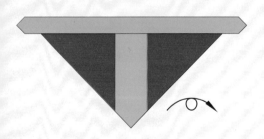

5. Turn over.

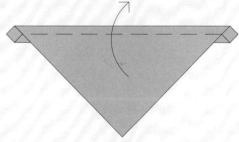

6. Valley fold.

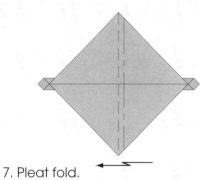

7. Pleat fold.

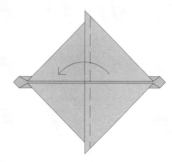

8. Valley fold in half.

9. Valley fold.

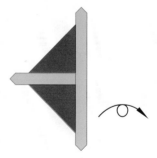

10. Turn over.

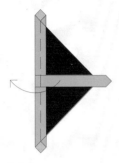

11. Valley fold.

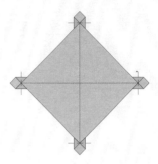

12. Make valley folds.

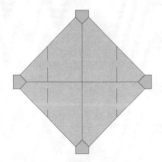

13. Make valley folds.

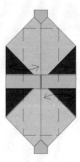

14. Make valley folds, then unfold two side folds only.

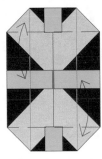

15. Make valley folds, then unfold.

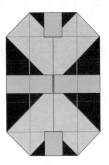

16. Completed step 15.

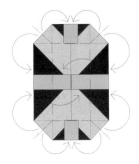

17. Pinch at the four corners and fold upward.

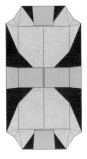

18. Appearance before completion.

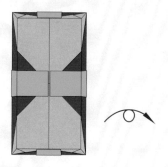

19. Turn over.

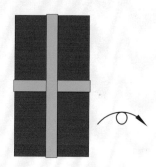

20. Rotate.

21. Completed assembly piece.

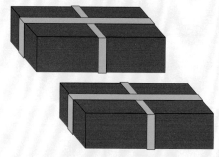

22. Repeat steps 1 through 20 for a second assembly piece.

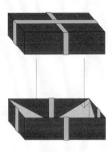

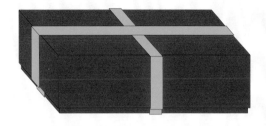

1. Join together the first and second assembly pieces as shown.

2. Completed Gift Box.

❄ INDEX